TWEETABLE
D. L. MOODY

Infotainment Press

Tweetable D. L. Moody: Quips, Quotes & Other One-Liners

Copyright © 2021 by Infotainment Press

All rights reserved. No portion of this book may be reproduced, stored in a retrieval system, or transmitted in any form or by any means—electronic, mechanical, photocopy, recording, scanning, or other—except for brief quotations in critical reviews or articles, without the prior written permission of the publisher.

Unless otherwise noted, Scripture quotations are taken from THE HOLY BIBLE, KING JAMES VERSION.

TWEETABLE
D. L. MOODY

QUIPS, QUOTES & OTHER ONE-LINERS

Right now I'm having so much trouble with D. L. Moody, that I don't have time to criticize my friends.

Seeking to perpetuate one's name on earth is like writing on the sand . . . to be perpetual it must be written on eternal shores.

Do you believe the Lord will call a poor sinner, and then cast him out? No!

A man does not get grace till he comes down to the ground, till he sees he needs grace.

There is no use trying to do Church work without love.

All those who have made a deep impression on the world, and have shined most brightly, have been those who lived in a dark day.

We talk about heaven being so far away. It is within speaking distance to those who belong there.

There would not be a harlot walking the streets, if it were not for unbelief.

Whatever the Lord does, He does it well.

There is no harder lesson to learn than the lesson of humility. It is not taught in the schools of men, only in the school of Christ.

My friends, even if you can't do much, show to which side you belong.

If a man could have saved himself, Christ would never have come into the world.

I think we shall find a great many of our prayers that we thought unanswered answered when we get to heaven.

*M*an has had no rest since Adam fell, and there is none for him until he returns to God again.

A good example is far better than a good precept.

*N*ow we have to take the Word of God just as it is; we have no authority to take out just what we like.

We have in our churches a great deal of prayer, but I think it would be a good thing if we had a praise meeting occasionally.

I believe the reason why so few find Christ is that they do not search for Him with all their hearts.

Prayer is a serious thing. We may be taken at our words.

The trouble is, people do not know that Christ is a Deliverer.

Other people want to love everything, and so they give up much of the truth; but we are to hold the truth in love.

God condemns the world because they believe not on Him; that is the root of all evil.

The billows may come surging and rolling up against us, but if we find refuge and shelter under Jesus Christ we have peace.

If I love the Lord Jesus Christ, little things are not going to separate me from His people. They are like the dust in the balance.

You think you cannot do much. If you are the means of saving one soul, that person may be instrumental in saving a hundred more.

If you probe the human heart, you will find a want, and that want is rest.

I believe that many a time trouble and sorrow are permitted to come to us that we may trust in Him alone.

Think of a place where temptation cannot come. Think of a place where we shall be free from sin and where the righteous shall reign.

*I*f the world has nothing to say against us,
we can be pretty sure that the Lord
Jesus Christ has very little to say for us.

All the devil's mountains are mountains of smoke.

But love is the only badge by which the disciples of our Lord Jesus Christ are known.

Preparation for old age should begin no later than one's teens.

No man in the world should be so happy as a man of God. It is one continual source of gladness.

How true that in the world we have tribulation . . .
 But within, peace may reign undisturbed.
 If sorrow is our lot, peace is our legacy.

It is easier for me to have faith in the Bible than in
 D.L. Moody, for Moody has fooled me many times.

I tell you whenever a man stands by God,
 God will stand by him.

Careful for nothing, prayerful for everything, thankful
 for anything.

I do not believe there has ever been a tear shed for sin since Adam's fall in Eden to the present time, but God has witnessed that.

The Bible was not given to increase our knowledge but to change our lives.

God will take you by the right hand and lead you through this wilderness, over death, and take you right into His kingdom.

Enthusiasm. We need more enthusiasm. The more we have, the better.

You had better play with forked lightning or meddle with the most deadly disease, than trifle with the Word of God.

Nothing that we do for God is small.

Take Christ's death and resurrection out of the New Testament, and you take out the key to the whole gospel of Jesus Christ.

David was the last one we would have chosen to fight the giant, but he was chosen of God.

When God says He will do a thing, there is no power on earth or in perdition that can keep Him from doing that.

Are you overcoming the world,
    or is the world overcoming you?

If God has sent you and me with a message it is not for us to say whether others will believe it or not. We cannot make men believe.

The longest time man has to live has no more proportion to eternity than a drop of dew has to the ocean.

Perseverance. The men who have been successful are not those who work by fits and starts, but three hundred and 65 days in the year.

Men full of the Spirit can look right into heaven.

If sometime you should read that D. L. Moody is dead, don't believe a word of it. He has gone up higher that is all.

All should work and ask God's guidance.

Faith is to work and trust, but hope is to wait and trust, to wait and expect; in other words, that hope is the daughter of faith.

His is not a creed, a mere doctrine, but it is He Himself we have.

Are you cultivating an unforgiving spirit? That is the spirit of the murderer, and needs to be rooted out of your heart.

Thank God for the privilege we have of confessing Christ.

Word and Work make healthy Christians. if we first study the Word and then go to work, we shall be healthy, useful Christians.

When we have Him with us, it will not be hard for us. Then the service of Christ will be delightful.

You have got a circle of friends. Go and tell them of Him.

The atheist says that he does not believe in God; he denies His existence, but he can't help setting up some other god in His place.

How many are worshiping gold today! Where war has slain its thousands, gain has slain its millions.

Earth and hell did all they could to keep that body in the grave; but they could not do it.

The man who is filled with his own Ideas refers rarely to the Word of God.

Prayer for the work of God will soon arouse your own sympathy and effort.

It is not what I think, nor what I feel, nor what I have done, but it is what Jesus Christ is and has done.

But if we have the peace of God, the world cannot take that from us.

The whole world doesn't amount to much, if you have not eternal life with it, to enjoy yourself in the future.

He went down into the grave and conquered it, and came up out of it; and now He says, "Because I live, you shall live also."

We can stand affliction better than we can prosperity, for in prosperity we forget God.

Oh! How many times I have thanked God that I gave up my will and took God's will.

If a man just stops to think what he has to praise God for, he will find there is enough to keep him singing praises for a week.

God's ways are not our ways. If He is going to work, we must let Him act as He pleases.

The mightiest man that ever lived could not deliver himself from his sins.

We cannot be too frequent in our requests. God will not weary of His children's prayers.

There is not such a great difference between grace and glory after all. Grace is glory begun, and glory is grace perfected.

Light for every darkness, life in death, the promise of our Lord's return, and the assurance of everlasting glory.

Where one man reads the Bible, a hundred read you and me.

If we are full of pride and conceit and ambition and self-seeking and pleasure and the world, there is no room for God.

The prayer of the humble and the contrite heart is a delight to God.

Now is the time to be saved.

Many men want a religion in which there is no cross, but they cannot enter heaven that way.

For many years I have never given an address without the consciousness that the Lord may come before I have finished.

If you get eternal life it is worth more than the whole world.

Character is what a man is in the dark.

Joy flows right on through trouble. Joy flows on through the dark. Joy flows in the night as well as in the day.

*T*here cannot be any peace
where there is uncertainty.

There is no better book with which to defend the Bible than the Bible itself.

If the glories of heaven are real, it will be to His praise and to our advantage to share in His rejection now.

We are good at confessing other people's sins, but if it is true repentance, we shall look after our own.

People are satisfied when you preach about the sins of the patriarchs, but they don't like it when you touch upon the sins of today.

I wish we had a few more women like the woman of Samaria, willing to confess what the Lord Jesus Christ had done for their souls.

The most solemn truth in the gospel is that the only thing Christ left down here is His blood.

Let us seek to be useful.

There was never a sermon which you have listened to but in it Christ was seeking for you.

The more we know God, the more we love Him. A great many of us would love God more if we only became better acquainted with Him.

Your heart may be overflowing with corruption and wickedness; yet Jesus will have compassion upon you.

If I can get a man to think seriously about death for five minutes, I can get him saved.

There is not one whom He cannot use, if we are willing to be used.

Let us be willing to do little things. And let us remember that nothing is small in which God is the source.

Faith is the foundation of all society. We have only to look around and see this.

When our prayers for earthly things are not answered, let us submit to the will of God, and know that it is all right.

If we are going to do a great work for God, we must spend much time in prayer; we have got to be closeted with God.

I believe in my soul that there are more at this day being lost for want of decision than for any other thing.

*W*hatever it costs us, let us be true Christians. It is like the dust in the balance in comparison to what God has in store for us.

*T*he more you love the Scriptures, the firmer will be your faith. There is little backsliding when people love the Scriptures.

*J*esus Christ came to save not good people, not the upright and just, but sinners like you and me who have gone astray.

There are some riches that never pass away. They are the treasures laid up in Heaven for those who truly belong to God.

If you pray for bread and bring no basket to carry it, you prove the doubting spirit.

Confession implies humility, and this, in God's sight, is of great price.

We should trust in Him who is our strength, and whose strength will never fail.

The beginning of greatness is to be little; the increase of greatness is to be less; the perfection of greatness is to be nothing.

I am only one, but I am one. I cannot do everything, but I can do something.

My friend, be wise! Make up your mind that you will seek the kingdom of God now.

Go take your story to him, and he will comfort you, and bind up and heal your sorrow.

You may find hundreds of faultfinders among professed Christians; but all their criticism will not lead one soul to Christ.

The best way to show a stick is crooked is not to argue or spend time denouncing it, but to lay a straight stick alongside it.

If you come into closer contact with the Word, you will gain something that will last, because the Word of God is going to endure.

There is no man living that can do the work that God has got for me to do.

*A*ll you have got to do is to prove that you are a sinner, and I will prove that you have got a Savior.

To fear is to have more faith in your antagonist than in Christ.

If we read the Word and do not pray, we may become puffed up with knowledge, without the love that buildeth up.

Experience has taught me that men who have very slight conviction of sin sooner or later lapse back into their old life.

If we were all of us doing the work that God has got for us to do, don't you see how the work of the Lord would advance?

Many a professing Christian is a stumbling-block because his worship is divided.

As you look into that face, as you look into those wounds on His feet or His hands, will you say He has not the power to save you?

There would not be a murderer, if it was not for unbelief, it is the germ of all sin.

Most anyone can sing in the morning when everything is bright and going well; but hope sings in the dark, in the mist and the fog.

Take your stand on the Rock of Ages. Let death, let the judgment come: the victory is Christ's and yours through Him.

Next to the wonder of seeing my Savior will be, I think, the wonder that I made so little use of the power of prayer.

It seems a poor empty life to live for the sake of self.

Out of 100 men, one will read the Bible, the other 99 will read the Christian.

From beginning to end, the Bible calls for whole-hearted allegiance to Him. There is to be no compromise with other gods.

Set your heart on what God has given you to do and don't be so foolish as to let your own difficulties stand in the way.

Faith is love on the battlefield.

All that you want to do is to cry, "God have mercy upon me," and you will receive the blessing.

A soul must be born before it can see light.

The Lord delights in hearing His children make their requests known unto Him—telling their troubles all out to Him.

I hold to the doctrine of sudden conversion as I do to my life, and I would as quickly give up my life as give up this doctrine.

I have never seen a dying saint who was rich in heavenly treasures who had any regret.

I'd rather be able to pray than to be a great preacher.

Dear sinners, Jesus is ready and willing to carry you over the mountains of sin and over your mountains of unbelief.

There is no knowledge like that of a man who knows he is saved, who can look up and see his "title clear to mansions in the skies".

You ask me why God loves. You might as well ask me why the sun shines. It can't help shining.

*You've got to get people lost
 before you can get them saved.*

As long as our mind is stayed on our dear selves,
we will never have peace.

There is a terrible battle going on now, and by-and-by,
when the war is over, God will call us home.

How people get on without the God of the Bible is
a mystery to me.

If you call on God for deliverance and for victory
over sin and every evil, God isn't going to turn
a deaf ear to your call.

If a man is not willing to go to heaven by the way of Calvary, he cannot go at all.

My friends, if you want any evidence, take God's word for it. You can't find better evidence than that.

Remember a small light will do a good deal when it is in a very dark place.

Unless your religion can keep you honest in your business, it isn't worth much.

Men think they are a great deal better than their fathers were. That suits human nature, for it is full of pride.

Church attendance is as vital to a disciple as a transfusion of rich, healthy blood to a sick man.

I feel that Jesus Christ ought to have a far better representative than I am.

The Lord gives His people perpetual joy when they walk in obedience to Him.

The tendency of the world is down—God's path is up.

Let every professed Christian ask, Where am I in the sight of God? Is my heart loyal to the King of heaven?

Christ showed Himself more than man by what He did. The Bible shows itself more than a human book by what it says.

Don't be kept out of active Christian work by the scorn and laughter and ridicule of your neighbors and companions.

After love comes peace.

Is your heart set upon God alone? If men were true to this commandment, obedience to the remaining nine would follow naturally.

[People] forget that the Son of God came to keep them from sin as well as to forgive it.

Some men tell us they don't have time to pray . . . if any man has God's work lying deep in his heart he will have time to pray.

More depends on my walk than talk.

No matter how great the work . . . how many difficulties had to be encountered, when they were sent from God they were sure to succeed.

I am tired and sick of half-heartedness. I don't like a half-hearted man. I don't care for anyone to love me half-heartedly.

By the grace of God, I'll be that man.

Salvation is worth working for.

A man who believes in the Lord Jesus Christ won't murder, and lie, and do all these awful things.

Merely reading the Bible is no use at all without we study it thoroughly, and hunt it through, as it were, for some great truth.

My friends, look to Christ, and not to yourselves.

Nothing the Savior found when He was on this earth pleased Him so as to see the faith of His disciples.

It isn't necessary to leave the things of this life when you follow Him.

He has been looking for you and hunting for you from your cradle. I will tell you how He seeks.

God has cast our confessed sins into the depths of the sea, and He's even put a 'No Fishing' sign over the spot.

Temptations are never so dangerous as when they come to us in a religious garb.

It is our privilege to know that we are saved.

My friends, if you go to the Lord with your troubles, He will take them away.

Earth recedes, heaven opens. I've been through the gates! Don't call me back . . . if this is death, it's sweet.

If there is a soul goes down to hell, it must go over God's love. You have to trample that love under your feet.

Love is the badge that Christ gave His disciples.

Every dart Satan can fire at us we can quench by faith. By faith we can overcome the Evil One.

The Christian on his knees sees more than the philosopher on tiptoe.

People want something to do for their salvation. God must do it all.

God doesn't seek for golden vessels, and does not ask for silver ones, but He must have clean ones.

There is not a better evangelist in the world than the Holy Spirit.

Peace is love in repose.

If Satan allows us to work unhindered, it is because our work is of no consequence.

If He bore the cross and died on it for me,
   ought I not to be willing to take it up for Him?

When we find a man meditating on the words
   of God, my friends, that man is full of boldness
   and is successful.

He that overcometh shall inherit all things.
   God has no poor children.

Christ was sent into the world to heal
   the broken-hearted.

Bring your sins, and He will bear them away into the wilderness of forgetfulness, and you will never see them again.

The world doesn't satisfy and if we can show the world that Jesus Christ does satisfy us, it will be more powerful than eloquent words.

Now there are a great many that have got truth, but they don't hold it in love, and they are very unsuccessful in working for God.

Heaven is not so far away but that God can hear us when we pray.

God commands us to be filled with the Spirit, and if we are not filled, it is because we are living beneath our privileges.

A man can no more take in a supply of grace for the future than he can eat enough today to last him for the next 6 months.

Work as if everything depended on you and pray as if everything depended on God.

Our greatest fear should not be of failure, but of succeeding at something that doesn't really matter.

If you can't see His way past the tears, trust His heart.

He is a faithful friend—a friend that sticketh closer than a brother.

If we are going to seek for Him and find Him, we must do it with all our hearts.

When a man is not deeply convicted of sin, it is a pretty sure sign that he has not truly repented.

It is not for me to sit down and wait for faith to come stealing over me . . . but is for me to take God at His Word.

We may be in darkness, but He is able to lead us in the right path. He is the Shepherd of His flock.

That which is born of the flesh may die. That which is born of the Spirit shall live forever.

Have faith in God! Take Him at His word!

If any man, woman, or child by a godly life and example can win one soul to God, his life will not have been a failure.

One of the most precious truths in the Word of God is that our Christ is not dead. He is risen.

Until conviction of sin brings us down on both knees, until we have no hope in ourselves left, we cannot find the Savior.

Long-suffering is love enduring.

My friends, it is a sweet privilege to pray, to be in touch with heaven, to be in communion with the great God.

I would rather die than live as I once did, a mere nominal Christian, and not used by God in building up His kingdom.

*W*orldly riches never make any one truly happy. We all know, too, that they often take wings and fly away.

A rule I have had for years is: to treat the Lord Jesus Christ as a personal friend.

*G*od will honor our faith.

Where I was born and where and how I have lived is unimportant. It is what I have done that should be of interest.

It is the greatest pleasure of living to win souls to Christ.

If I take care of my character, my reputation will take care of me.

No man can resolve himself into Heaven.

Lighthouses don't fire cannons to call attention to their shining—they just shine.

I don't care where it is, what part of the world it's in, if we have a praise church we'll have successful Christianity.

And when he says "Preach the gospel to every creature," every creature can be saved if he will.

If you accept His offer, from the clouds of your transgressions you shall be lifted into the Heaven of joy and peace.

The love of God is as the mighty ocean in its greatness, dwelling with and flowing from God's Spirit.

God has had one Son without sin, but He has never had one without sorrow.

A man who prays much in private will make short prayers in public.

We are not reaching the world, because the church itself has become conformed to the world and worldly-minded.

If a man has got the Word, he must speak or die.

A false hope is worse than no hope. Make up your mind that you will not rest until you reach a hope that is worth having.

I would rather a thousand times be five minutes at the feet of Christ than listen a lifetime to all the wise men in the world.

The true believer prizes heaven above everything else, and is willing to give up the world.

𝒫eople think God does not like to be troubled with our constant coming and asking. The only way to trouble God is not to come at all.

One of two things you must do; you must either receive Him or reject Him.

I do not know anything that would wake up Chicago better than for every man and woman here who loves Him to begin to talk about Him.

Faith is an outward look. Faith does not look within; it looks without.

The way of obedience is always the way of blessing.

When a man has no strength, if he leans on God, he becomes powerful.

A great many people seem to embalm their troubles. I always feel like running away when I see them coming.

The hour had come for Christ to conquer Death, for that was what he went into the grave for.

We are always in the majority when we are with God.

*I*f we are truly children of God our names have gone on before, and there will be a place awaiting us at the end of the journey.

*T*here is no greater honor than to be the instrument in God's hands of leading one person into the glorious light of Heaven.

*L*ove will rebuke evil, but will not rejoice in it. Love will be impatient of sin, but patient with the sinner.

I do not believe there is a spot where peace can be found except under the shadow of the cross.

Now let us hold the truth, but let us hold it in love. People will stand almost any kind of plain talk if you only do it in love.

If we pray without reading the Word, we shall become mystical and fanatical, and liable to be blown about by every wind of doctrine.

You receive Him here and He will receive you there; you reject Him here and He will reject you there.

Jesus Christ never taught his disciples how to preach, but only how to pray.

*L*ove is the badge by which the disciples of our Lord Jesus Christ are known.

*T*he cross is the center. Bring people nigh to it and you bring them nigh to each other.

*I*f you know the truth in Christ, there need be no fear, because death will only hasten you on to glory.

*E*verything He promised to do, He is able and willing to accomplish.

It is a masterpiece of the devil to make us believe that
children cannot understand religion.

Man might do that, but God never mocks men.

When Jesus Christ enlists someone in His service . . .
He lets him know that he must live a life of self-denial.

The brightest home on earth is but an empty barn,
compared with the mansions that are in the skies.

I have had more trouble with myself
than with any other man.

Whatever you make most of is your god. Whatever you love more than God is your idol.

I cannot choose for myself as well as God can choose for me, and it is much better to surrender my will to God's will.

The Holy Spirit takes the things of Christ and brings them to our mind. He testifies of Christ; He guides us into the truth about Him.

You say "I am afraid I cannot hold out." Well, Christ will hold out for you.

If we can't take time during the week, we will have Sunday uninterrupted.

Treat the Lord Jesus Christ as a personal friend. His is not a creed, a mere doctrine, but it is He Himself we have.

Now if I have got the spirit of Christ, then it is that I have got a power that is greater than any power in the world.

We cannot work for God without love. It is the only tree that can produce fruit on this sin-cursed earth that is acceptable to God.

A life which is empty of purpose until 65 will not suddenly become filled on retirement.

Man is born with his face turned away from God. When he truly repents, he is turned around toward God; he leaves his old life.

The grace of God hath power to bring salvation to all men, and if a man is unsaved it is because he wants to work it out.

Depend upon it, my friends, if you get tired of the Word of God, and it becomes wearisome to you, you are out of communion with Him.

If Christ comes into our hearts we are not ashamed.

Take those Christians who are rooted and grounded in the Word of God, and you will find they have great peace.

When a man stoops to the dust and acknowledges that he needs mercy, then it is that the Lord will give him grace.

A man can counterfeit love, faith, hope and all the other graces, but it is very difficult to counterfeit humility.

Joy is love exalted.

Thanks be to God, there is hope today; this very hour you can choose Him and serve Him.

It is not necessary to give up your business, if it's a legitimate one, in order to accept Christ.

Some little act of kindness will perhaps do more to influence people than any number of long sermons.

People are always looking in their own hearts to get freedom; but it is the truth which makes us free—the Word of God.

Nothing can offend those who trust in Christ.

Death may be the King of terrors, but Jesus is the King of kings!

The very things we do not like are sometimes the very best for us.

I contend that a man cannot but find in every page of this book that Jesus Christ is seeking him through His blessed Word.

Gentleness is love in society.

And if the work ain't done we will have to answer for it when we stand before God's bar.

Families who marry for wealth, and marry the godly to the ungodly, always bring distress into the family.

If He seems not to come to us in our affliction,
    it is only to test us.

Prayer means that I am to be raised up into feeling,
    into union and design with him.

You will find, my friends, that there is no class of people
    exempt from broken hearts.

Give me a man who says this one thing I do,
    and not those fifty things I dabble in.

I was born of the flesh in 1837.
    I was born of the Spirit in 1856.

Let us pray, and as we pray, let us make room for Jesus in our hearts.

I do not believe there is any true revival that is not brought about by a good deal of prayer.

Believing and confessing go together; and you cannot be saved without them both.

The sweetest lesson I have learned in God's school is to let the Lord choose for me.

There is no hope for a man until he sees that he is under just condemnation for his sins.

If we have got the true love of God shed abroad in our hearts we will show it in our lives.

We ought to see the face of God every morning before we see the face of man.

Unless the Spirit of God is with us, we cannot expect that our prayers will be answered.

The preaching that this world needs most is the sermons in shoes that are walking with Jesus Christ.

Humility consists not in thinking meanly of ourselves, but in not thinking of ourselves at all.

When men learn the lesson that they are nothing and God is everything, then there is not a position in which God cannot use them.

Even though it were in my power to say, 'My will be done', I would rather say to Him, 'Thy will be done'.

God has sent us into the world to shine for Him—to light up this dark world.

God will not desert us in our time of need, any more than He deserted His people of old when they were hard pressed by their foes.

Christ is the remedy of sin. What you want is to look from the wound to the remedy—to Jesus, the Author and Finisher of our faith.

However great our difficulties, or deep even our sorrows, there is room for thankfulness.

No man who has ever been sent by God to do His work has ever failed.

If you say "I will fast when God lays it on my heart" you never will. You are too cold and indifferent to take the yoke upon you.

We are apt to rush into God's presence, and rush out again, without any real sense of the reverence and awe that is due Him.

I have never heard such a one say he had lived too much for God and heaven.

Let us have one day exclusively to study and read the Word of God.

Now the question is, "Shall we have a great and mighty harvest, or shall we go on discussing our differences?"

Yes, thank God, He has conquered Death and the grave; and you can shout now, "O grave, where is thy victory?"

Small numbers make no difference to God. There is nothing small if God is in it.

Real true faith is man's weakness leaning on God's strength.

No man ever lost his life with Him.

It is an unceasing fountain bubbling up in the heart; a secret spring the world can't see and doesn't know anything about.

Human eloquence or persuasiveness of speech are the mere trappings of the dead, if the living Spirit be absent.

The Spirit of God first imparts love; he next inspires hope, and then gives liberty.

If you give way to little temptations, you will not be able to resist when great temptations come to you.

Let us pray that God may carry on a deep and thorough work, that people may be convicted of sin so that they cannot rest in unbelief.

My faith bows down before the inspired Word and I unhesitatingly believe the great things of God when even the intellect is confused.

The Bible was not given for our information but for our transformation.

Every good gift that we have had from the cradle up has come from God.

The Bible will keep you from sin, or sin will keep you from the Bible.

If there is anything that ought to make heaven near to Christians, it is knowing that God and all their loved ones will be there.

When temper gets the mastery over me I am its slave, and it is a source of weakness.

I firmly believe a great many prayers are not answered because we are not willing to forgive someone.

The unregenerate man likes heaven better than hell, but he likes this world the best of all.

Shame on the Christianity of the nineteenth century; it's a weak and sickly thing.

Here we read of the ruin of man by nature, redemption by the blood, and regeneration by the Holy Ghost.

God has not left it for us to do; all we have to do is to enter into it.

If you are under the power of evil, and you want to get under the power of God, cry to Him to bring you over to His service.

He came to deliver us from our sinful dispositions, and create in us pure hearts.

I believe there is no man in the world so constituted but he can believe in God's word.

This earth, if we are Christians, is not our home; it is up yonder.

One drop of God's strength is worth more than all the world.

The fiercer the battle the young believer is called on to wage, the surer evidence it is of the work of the Holy Spirit.

It is a good thing to lose confidence in ourselves so as to gain confidence in God.

If we let some false god come in and steal our love away from the God of heaven, we shall have no peace.

Would you not rather be with the Lord and get rid of your troubles, than be with your troubles and without God?

Some people hold the truth, but in such a cold stern way that it will do no good.

The valley of the shadow of death holds no darkness for the child of God.

Never think that Jesus commanded a trifle, nor dare to trifle with anything He has commanded.

Christ never preached any funeral sermons.

And none will ever seek to be delivered until they get their eyes open and see that they have been taken captive.

The resurrection is the keystone of the arch on which our faith is supported.

*N*othing will break the stubborn heart
so quickly as the love of Christ.

God sends no one away empty except those who are full of themselves.

A holy life will produce the deepest impression.

When a messenger of Christ begins to change the message because he thinks that he is wiser than God, God just dismisses that man.

Spread out your petition before God, and then say, "Thy will, not mine, be done."

I have never yet known the Spirit of God to work where the Lord's people were divided.

*F*aith takes God without any ifs.

*M*oses was the very man that God wanted, and when he met God with the question "Who am I?" it didn't matter who he was but who his God was.

*J*oy flows all through persecution and opposition, for it is an unceasing fountain bubbling in the heart.

If you believe on the Lord Jesus Christ you are free.

And if their hearts were there (heaven) their minds would be up there, and their lives would tend toward heaven.

The nearer we get to God, the more we have to throw out of the things of this world.

We are permitted to draw upon God's store of grace from day to day as we need it.

Heaven is a prepared place for a prepared people.

It is folly for anyone to attempt to fight in his own strength. The world, the flesh and the devil are too much for any man.

But if we are linked to Christ by faith, and He is formed in us the hope of glory, then we shall get the victory over every enemy.

A man who has not realized what the blood has done for him has not the token of salvation.

I cannot see into the future as God can; therefore, it is a good deal better to let Him choose for me than to choose for myself.

We can rely on what Christ says, and He says, 'He that believeth on Me shall not perish, but have everlasting life.'

A doctor, a lawyer, may do good work without love, but God's work cannot be done without love.

[*T*here are] people that love so much that they give up the truth because they are afraid it will hurt some one's feelings.

You cannot find a case in the Bible where a man has been honest in dealing with sin, but God has been honest with him and blessed him.

I would rather have my life hid with Christ in God than be in Eden as Adam was.

Before we pray that God would fill us, I believe we ought to pray that He would empty us.

I am quite convinced of this, that God knows better what is best for me and for the world than I can possibly know.

*T*he world cannot, and never could,
satisfy a hungry soul.

We shall draw the world to Christ when we are filled with religion.

If we want anything at all that we cannot get, that is a kind of poverty. Sometimes the richer the man the greater the poverty.

Go and do a good turn for that person of whom you are jealous. That is the way to cure jealousy; it will kill it.

It will not come hard to people who are serving God down here to do it when they go up yonder.

We cannot serve God, we cannot work for God unless we have love. That is the key which unlocks the human heart.

Every great movement of God can be traced to a kneeling figure.

We may easily be too big for God to use, but never too small.

Oh, young man, character is worth more than money, character is worth more than anything else in this wide world.

Many are sorry for their sins, sorry that they cannot continue in sin; but they repent only with hearts that are not broken.

What God wants you to do is to use the influence you have.

Keep us little and unknown, prized and loved by God alone.

Death didn't take Jesus into the grave; he followed Death into his own dominion and bound him hand and foot, and came up victorious.

Meekness is love in school.

Do you think there is a heart so bruised and broken that can't be healed by Him?

Those who say they will forgive but can't forget, bury the hatchet, but they leave the handle out for immediate use.

When they were sent from God they were sure to succeed.

Attitudes determine our actions, for good or bad.

If you take my advice, you will have no will other than God's will.

There is nothing on this earth that pleases Christ so much as faith.

God will have a man humble himself down on his face before Him, with not a word to say for himself.

No sooner has a soul escaped from his snare than the great Adversary takes steps to ensnare it again.

Lust is the devil's counterfeit of love.

There is no sin in the whole catalogue of sins you can name but Christ will deliver you from it perfectly.

Why is it that many Christians are cold? Because they are all the time receiving, never giving out anything.

We are told to let our light shine, and if it does, we won't need to tell anybody it does.

You don't have to go to heathen lands today to find false gods. America is full of them.

We are led on by an unseen power that we have not got strength to resist, or else we are led on by the loving Son of God.

If you want the blessings of heaven, take your stand at once for Him.

Those who have left the deepest impression on this sin-cursed earth have been men and women of prayer.

Next to the might of God, the serene beauty of a holy life is the most powerful influence of good in all the world.

When a man is filled with the Word of God you cannot keep him still.

A nobody with God can be a somebody.

*I*f you receive Him it will be well; if you reject Him and are lost it will be terrible.

We must not limit the mighty grace of God.

If your own name is in the Book of Life, let your next aim in life be to get the children whom God has given you there also.

The world can get on very well without you and me, but the world cannot get on without Christ.

I would not give much for all that can be done by sermons, if we do not preach Christ by our lives.

He who kneels the most, stands the best.

I believe Satan to exist for two reasons: first, the Bible says so; and second, I've done business with him.

Many times we go against our feelings. Faith is one thing, feeling is another.

Every man, I don't care who he is—even the strongest—every man that hasn't Christ in him, is a failure.

His is a loving, tender hand, full of sympathy and compassion.

I know the Bible is inspired because it inspires me.

He is at the right hand of God; and where can He be to carry on His work any better than up yonder?

There is peace for the conscience through His blood, and peace for the heart in His love.

The man that is popular with the world is not a friend of Jesus. You cannot serve two masters.

If we have a praise church we will have people converted.

If we could only get people to praise God for what He has done, it would be better than asking Him continually for something.

When we are living in the light of our Savior we shine with His light.

God has called us to shine, just as much as Daniel was sent into Babylon to shine.

Would Christ have made a child the standard of faith if He had known that it was not capable of understanding His words?

Moses said, "Who am I?" He was very small in his own eyes—just small enough so that God could use him.

He can heal them all, but the great trouble is that men won't come.

Don't let Satan deceive you. Nearly everything around tends to draw us away from God.

When we know our Bible:
then it is that God can use us.

There is no mountain that He will not climb with you if
you will; He will deliver you from your besetting sin.

A creed is the road or street. It is very good as far as it
goes, but if it doesn't take us to Christ it is worthless.

Looking at the wound of sin will never save anyone.
What you must do is look at the remedy.

The law tells me how crooked I am. Grace comes along and straightens me out.

Praise is not only speaking to the Lord on our own account, but it is praising Him for what He has done for others.

When God wants to move a mountain, he does not take a bar of iron, but he takes a little worm.

Some Christians are only good in spots, because they do not take in the whole sweep of the Scriptures.

The prophet may preach to the bones in the valley, but it must be the breath from Heaven which will cause the slain to live.

It is not a sin to be tempted; the sin is to fall into temptation.

Let trouble come if it will drive us nearer to God.

A rule I follow is to treat the Lord Jesus Christ as a personal friend. He is not a creed or doctrine, but it is He Himself we have.

Every temptation you overcome makes you stronger to overcome others, while every temptation that defeats you makes you weaker.

God has nothing to say to the self-righteous.

He will speak comforting words to you; not treat you coldly or spurn you, as perhaps those of earth would.

Peace has already been made by the Cross. Christ has made peace for us, and now what He desires is that we enter into it.

God will speak to him, when he owns that he is a sinner, and gets rid of all his own righteousness.

I don't care how you have back-slid and wandered; if you really want to come back, God will hear your prayer, and answer.

Every one of our children will be brought into the ark, if we pray and work earnestly for them.

When the dying hour comes, there will be dying grace; but you do not require dying grace to live by.

$\mathcal{T}$here are many of us that are willing to do great things for the Lord, but few of us are willing to do little things.

The blood of Jesus Christ cleanses from all sin . . . we Christians ought to be the happiest people in the world.

God's honor is something worth seeking. Man's honor doesn't amount to much.

If I walk with the world, I can't walk with God.

You may be sure that something is wrong with you when everybody is your friend.

Grace means undeserved kindness. It is the gift of God to man the moment he sees he is unworthy of God's favor.

Faith makes all things possible . . . love makes all things easy.

Every new discovery must necessarily raise in us a fresh sense of the greatness, wisdom, and power of God.

Let no one say that he cannot shine because he has not so much influence as some others may have.

A man ought to live so that everybody knows he is a Christian . . . and most of all, his family ought to know.

Trust in yourself and you are doomed to disappointment . . . but trust in GOD, and you are never to be confounded in time or eternity.

What makes the Dead Sea dead? Because it is all the time receiving, never giving out anything.

Every one of us is met by the prince of this world and the Prince of Peace.

The reason why so many Christians fail all through life is just this—they underestimate the strength of the enemy.

One of the great obstacles in the way of God's work today is this want of love among those who are the disciples.

How far away is Heaven? It is not so far as some imagine.

I would rather go into the kingdom of heaven through the poor house than go down to hell in a golden chariot.

*T*he longer I live the more I am convinced that godly men and women are not appreciated in our day.

Let us seek to be vessels meet for the Master's use, that God, the Holy Spirit, may shine fully through us.

The best thing I ever did was when I surrendered my will, and let the will of God be done in me.

Now just think a moment and answer the question, "What shall I do with Jesus who is called Christ?"

I believe many a man is praying to God to fill him when he is full already with something else.

The law condemns me, but Christ has satisfied the claims of the law. He tasted death for every man.

If our circumstances find us in God, we shall find God in all our circumstances.

Let God have your life;
    He can do more with it than you can.

A man who is flattering himself that he is humble is self-deceived.

The voice of sin is loud, but the voice of forgiveness is louder.

Do you believe that He would send those men out to preach the gospel to every creature unless he wanted every creature to be saved?

Goodness is love in action.

The Bible without the Holy Spirit is a sundial by moonlight.

A great many people are trying to make peace, but that has already been done.

Things that look very large to us, look very small in heaven; and things that seem small down here, may be very great up yonder.

We cannot get on any better without hope than we can without faith.

And that which I can do, by the grace of God, I will do.

The impression that a praying mother leaves upon her children is life-long.

Rest cannot be found in the world, and thank God the world cannot take it from the believing heart!

The moment our hearts are emptied of selfishness and ambition and self-seeking . . . the Holy Spirit will come and fill our hearts.

God never made a promise that was too good to be true.

When the Spirit came upon the Son of Man, He gave His life; He healed the broken-hearted.

Temperance is love in training.

Sometimes you can brace yourself up against a great temptation; and almost before you know it you fall before some little thing.

The world does not understand theology or dogma, but it understands love and sympathy.

*T*emptations are like tramps. Treat them kindly, and they will return bringing others with them.

There must be light, else there could be no shadow. Jesus is the light. He has overcome death.

I believe the family was established long before the church, and my duty is to my family first. I am not to neglect my family.

Everyone of us can love Christ, and we can all do something for Him. It may be a small thing; but whatever it is it shall be lasting.

I would a thousand times rather that God's will should be done than my own.

When a man thinks he has got a good deal of strength, and is self-confident, you may look for his downfall.

You certainly cannot bring forth fruit to the honor and glory of God until you get self-control.

I would rather have the God of heaven for my Protector than all the armies of earth and all the navies of the world to protect me.

He simply tells you to believe in Him, and He will save you.

What a blessing it is to have such a Savior.

I cannot preach on hell unless I preach with tears.

God is not dead. He is as powerful, as willing, to help today as ever He was. Why, then, are we not full of faith in Him?

If a man loses wealth, character, reputation, he may gain it again; but oh, if he loses his soul, he can never regain it.

Oh, may we all find rest in Christ now!

If we do not love one another, we certainly shall not have much power with God in prayer.

We call things great that may look very small to Jesus Christ; and things that look very small to us may look very large to Him.

There is no sound that goes up from this sin-cursed earth so sweet to God's ear as the prayer of the man who is walking uprightly.

*T*his is a time of weeping, but by-and-by there will be a time when God shall call us where there will be no tears.

When Christians find themselves exposed to temptation they should pray to God to uphold them.

The world knows little of the works wrought by prayer.

It is my work to preach and hold up the Cross and testify of Christ; but it is His work to convict men of sin and lead them to Christ.

What is the price that you put upon your soul? You say you do not know. I will tell you. It is the sin that keeps you from God.

There must be no idol in the heart if we are going to do the will of God on earth.

No thief shall inherit the kingdom of God.

If He laid down His life for us, is it not the least we can do to lay down ours for Him?

No one can sum up all God is able to accomplish through one solitary life, wholly yielded, adjusted, and obedient to Him.

Take courage. We walk in the wilderness today and in the Promised Land tomorrow.

Between human love and divine love there is as much difference as there is between darkness and light.

He will comfort you as a mother comforts her child if you will only come in prayer and lay all your burdens before Him.

www.ingramcontent.com/pod-product-compliance
Lightning Source LLC
Chambersburg PA
CBHW061327040426
42444CB00011B/2805